FEEDING THE GHOSTS

FEEDING THE GHOSTS

POEMS

RAHUL MEHTA

UNIVERSITY PRESS OF KENTUCKY

Published by The University Press of Kentucky

Scholarly publisher for the Commonwealth, serving Bellarmine University, Berea College, Centre College of Kentucky, Eastern Kentucky University, The Filson Historical Society, Georgetown College, Kentucky Historical Society, Kentucky State University, Morehead State University, Murray State University, Northern Kentucky University, Spalding University, Transylvania University, University of Kentucky, University of Louisville, University of Pikeville, and Western Kentucky University. All rights reserved.

Editorial and Sales Offices: The University Press of Kentucky
663 South Limestone Street, Lexington, Kentucky 40508-4008
www.kentuckypress.com

Cataloging-in-Publication data available from the Library of Congress

ISBN 978-0-8131-9879-8 (hardcover)
ISBN 978-0-8131-9880-4 (paperback)
ISBN 978-0-8131-9881-1 (pdf)
ISBN 978-0-8131-9882-8 (epub)

This book is printed on acid-free paper meeting
the requirements of the American National Standard
for Permanence in Paper for Printed Library Materials.

Manufactured in the United States of America.

Member of the Association
of University Presses

for my parents
Kunj and Nalini Mehta
with devotion, love, and gratitude

for Michele Natasha Reese
(1973–2023)

CONTENTS

AUTHOR'S NOTE

Find the beauty.

This became my mantra in spring 2017, a difficult time. The political tensions of the country and the world, the existential threat of climate crisis, and my own personal and professional disappointments had left me raw.

That spring, the nine of wands kept showing up in my tarot. It's a card that says, *You are battered, you are weary, but keep fighting. And know: What are you fighting for?* I wasn't sure. I had to think. After some work, I realized that what I was fighting for that spring, that year, was the ability—amid my fear and outrage and anger and sorrow and disappointment—to see the world as beautiful.

It is a practice. I gave myself the daily task of finding one thing of beauty. It was usually something in nature: the color of the grass in the morning, a bird's nest hidden in the rafters of the train station, the mottled bark of the century-old sycamores outside our apartment building. Sometimes it was my dog sleeping quietly in the corner. Sometimes it was the sunlight on the windowsill. *Often* it was the sunlight on the windowsill.

The year 2020 and a global pandemic, followed in 2021 by a family member's cancer diagnosis, brought new challenges. This practice felt—feels—as urgent as ever.

The pieces here were all written over roughly five years, starting in spring 2017. They may not all seem immediately connected to the practice of finding beauty, but they are all borne out of it. Many dip into my past, growing up brown, the child of immigrants, and queer in West Virginia.

Messy beauty. Ugly beauty. This-is-my-truth beauty. *Find it. Find it all.*

It is a fight. I am still fighting. It is good to have something to fight for. It is good to know what you are fighting for.

I.

SWORDS

On a park bench, a woman in her sixties is telling a man in his sixties her life story. At least I think it's a woman in her sixties and a man in his sixties—I have never been good at guessing ages and I'm learning not to make assumptions about gender.

The woman's life story, though unremarkable, is enthralling (as are all life stories, when told truthfully). The listening makes it so.

The man is sipping something out of a bottle in a plastic bag. The woman is smoking cigarettes. She extinguishes them in the dirt with a kitten-heeled sandal.

At some point I realize they are on a date: not a first date, but maybe a fourth or fifth. They are testing whether they can be together this way for weeks, months, years.

Evening mist settles, softening the edges. It is still hot, and the trees are full and heavy. As the last remaining people leave, I hear owls, frogs, and squirrels calmly but persistently making their cases.

On the block print bedcover (hand-me-down from my parents) on which I've been sitting in the grass, I had drawn, perhaps an hour earlier, three tarot cards, all devastating, all swords, and with each I felt my body being pierced by blades so sharp I was surprised to find on the fabric no blood. One card I have been holding to my heart without realizing.

The woman and the man get up and start walking across the expanse of green, toward a small pond, and, beyond that, a thicket. They stroll arm-in-arm, very slowly, a bit unsteady: the man drunk, the woman in her kitten heels. They are both smiling.

As I watch them disappear deep into the darkening park, I start to tell myself my own life story. I've never before told it this way. My self has never before listened.

II.

PEN

My father,
an engineer,
always has
a ballpoint pen
in his shirt front pocket,
the kind that clicks
and whose black ink
smells of—how can I
describe it?—stopping
for gas after a long day's
drive, a check tucked
into a birthday
card, a bucket of water
sloshed across
the hot concrete
of a Bombay terrace,
crows watching from
the ledges.
When he writes,
his tongue finds
a corner of his mouth,
he chews
his lower lip,
he hunches his back
as though he's eight,
as though this act of making

marks, of shaping letters and
numbers and words, is still
hard work,
is mysterious and important,
is the key that opens
everything.

As a writer I've favored
fountain or felt-tip
or occasionally gel,
but never ballpoint,
but now I'm wondering
what if I did, what might
my poems become?
I imagine each stanza
as—though I cannot
explain this—a flock
of ravens (stop
saying *conspiracy,* stop
saying *unkindness*)
darkening the sky,
the remaining white spaces
a puzzle of their own.
I imagine the words
as shape-shifting bats
about to become
something else,
black-caped and fanged,
seductive and terrifying
and wanted.

And now the click
of the pen is the
click of the heels
of ruby slippers—
I am three
in my father's lap,
and he is writing
something, I don't
know what,
a mortgage coupon,
a to-do list on a
yellow pad,
notes for work,
chemical compounds,
complex formulas,
or, most likely—
on that impossibly
thin paper the blue of
the sky the day after
a storm, in Devanagari
script that rises and
falls and crashes
like waves—
an aerogram
home.

LAUNDRY DAY

My kurta hangs
from a hook on my fire escape
in Philadelphia:
pink against red brick
& a rust-colored door.
The breeze breathes
into it
life. It is
my elder cousin
taking me for the first time
to Gandhi's ashram,
saying to me *khadi,*
saying to me *swadeshi,*
saying *homespun* &
self-reliance &
nonviolent resistance,
teaching me past, present & future.
It is my uncle
in chappals
on the cracked concrete
patio
of our house in
West Virginia
when he first came
to America more than
forty years ago.

It is my grandfather
lost among racks of
plaid flannel shirts
at a JCPenney
in a small-town mall &
climbing the steps
at Babulnath &
making tea in a
two-room flat in
South Mumbai.
It is my father
at a baraat
outside the Pierre Hotel,
at a Navratri dandiya raas
in a rented community center
with a groaning water
fountain & wood paneling &
speckled floors.
It is me
at Kanniyakumari
where three oceans meet,
me at Point Park
where two rivers clash,
me in a cane chair
on a summer lawn in Alfred,
New York, &

me tomorrow
with my students
in Philadelphia
in a windowless classroom
high above Broad Street,
fifteen desk chairs
arranged in a circle,
pen across paper
or clicking keyboards,
the sound of
our stories
rising.

LAYING IT DOWN

The men
on the roof
of our building
listen to Spanish
music as they
work. Acoustic
guitar outlines
a plaintive melody
filled in by a voice
the color of
glowing coal. Nail
gun pulses;
circular saw
growls. One
of the workers
sings along,
not to the whole song,
but to a phrase
here & there.
His voice is not good,
not like the voice
on the recording,
but it is loud &
seems to come
from some-
where deep, & I think—
despite the hard work

of laying down roof—
it must feel nice
to be outside,
to be high
in the air & to
howl.
                Below,
I am working,
too, sitting at my
desk in my own
patch of sunlight,
sipping coffee from
a white mug
with blue & orange
sunflowers, writing
this poem. On
my desk, a
candle burns,
silly in such bright
sun, but I like
to light a candle
when I write &
so I have.
The gold
nib of my pen
scratches messy marks
across the white page—
my own croaking
howl—
the words
planks
for the ground
beneath me.

THE SECRET

Maybe today
is the day
I will learn
to care for
my photosynthesizing friends:
the asparagus fern
hanging in the front room,
the succulent in the small
white pot, the aloe
in the windowsill that has
twice been toppled by
strong gusts.
Given my negligence
it is a miracle
the asparagus fern—
gifted to us some twenty-two
years ago, soon after Robert
and I moved into our first
apartment together, a third
floor Brooklyn flat with low
stamped-tin ceilings that would
sizzle like skillets
come summer—has, if not
thrived, survived.
And who's to say
it isn't thriving

in its own way?
We don't all need
to flaunt our locks
or flip our hair
in choreographed waves
to hip-hop or metal
or bubblegum pop.
But I am making excuses.

The summer we spent away
in the desert and paid
a neighbor to water our plants,
we returned and I'd
never seen them so lush;
even the sickly bromeliad
bloomed.
The neighbor
and his girlfriend were hiding
their relationship from
her Sri Lankan mother
for fear she would not accept
her daughter dating a white
boy, never mind she herself had
married a white man, a professor
in the department where
she was chair.

Those some twenty-two
years ago, my father
drove a faux wood–paneled
minivan, a mattress strapped
to the roof, five hundred miles
from Parkersburg, West Virginia,

to Butler Street, Brooklyn,
and, while unloading
the vehicle, asked me, again and again—
though he knew Robert and I
were a couple, was, in fact,
fresh with this knowledge—
Which bedroom is yours?
He grumbled
about the flat, a
dump, and I wanted
to say, look! stamped-
tin ceilings! tall trees out front!
floorboards wide
as notebook paper! He said,
though he did not say this,
This is no way to live.

The neighbor who watered
our houseplants
that summer—a tattooed
classicist—now is an assistant
professor somewhere in Florida.
He and the girlfriend
married. His wife
never finished
her PhD at her top-ranked
program; she was being harassed—
sexually, racially—by a star faculty
member and now teaches
middle school. I don't know
how she eventually
told her mother.

What was the classicist's secret? I want
to know. I fill
an orange pitcher
and climb onto a chair.

MY BIRTHRIGHT

. . . pain was part of my birthright, part of what was meant by a word like Home.
FROM *ORDINARY LIGHT*, BY TRACY K. SMITH

FEAR IS MY BIRTHRIGHT

My father trod carefully, perhaps never fully believing this country was his. He didn't speak up, he didn't say no. He introduced himself by his initials only, made it easy, didn't make them form their mouths around foreign sounds, around hard, dark syllables, didn't ask that people say his name. I never made them say my name either, let them call me Chocolate Boy and Ragu, and, later, worse. I went quietly to my school locker, stored there my books, my pencils, and, in my magnetic mirror, my true reflection, and locked it all away.

SHAME IS MY BIRTHRIGHT

Because I imagined the towel wrapped around my eight-year-old body was a dress.

Because of the dolls, the Hello Kitty jewelry box, the Trapper Keeper with a big-eyed cotton ball kitten in a field of daisies.

Because when we played pretend, I said I was pretending to be James Bond but secretly I was pretending to be a Bond Girl.

19

Because many years later, when I told my mom about my then-boyfriend-now-partner, she said she hoped he wasn't one of those swishy gays, and I thought, *But I am one of those swishy gays*, then vowed to try my hardest not to be.

Because Vivek Shraya came to me in a dream recently—looking all kinds of Mahalaxmi glam—and gave me a bindi and a set of sparkly bangles and whispered, *Don't forget who you are*, but maybe I already have.

JOY IS MY BIRTHRIGHT

My tarot cards tell me
to be naked
make it a ritual
do it in public.

I want to tell about fire.

Nakedness
literal and metaphoric
terrifies me.

I want to tell about joy.

One. At the Korean baths last December
I was naked.
Two. Canoeing in the Adirondacks
five years ago
I was half-naked—
does that count?

Three. In Maine, last summer,
in the low tide cove, crouching in
the gray clay
that almost swallowed me whole,
I was naked. I was thinking
about Shiva.

I want to tell about fire.

I was thinking about Kali
last summer
when Mel and Christine
visited us in Philly
on the hottest weekend
in years
and we walked four miles
midday and collapsed
on a rock
on a cliff
above the creek
that breaks my heart.
Crick, my Appalachian self says.
The crick that bricks my heart.

I want to tell about joy.

I want to break my heart.

I want to tell about fire.

I want to brick my heart.

I want to tell about joy.

LET HER

Let her do
what she needs
to do, says
the tall woman
outside the café,
except that the *she*
in question is
my large, badly-
behaved dog
& what
she needs to do,
evidently, is
snarl & growl
& bark
at the woman
& I don't know if I
should pull her
away or distract her
with a mango-flavored
dog treat, or to—
as the woman has
instructed—*let her.* The
woman is wearing
a tight, mid-thigh,
leather-looking skirt
this weekday afternoon,

a boxy blouse
& lipstick the color
of crushed cranberries,
which is smeared
on the rim
of her white
paper cup.

& I don't know
if I should
mention here
that the woman
is trans (or
rather, that I
perceive her to
be trans, because
how would I know
for sure?), if
it is relevant to
the poem,
relevant to
anything,
& maybe to
even mention it is
to other her,

except that I noticed
it right away &
I can't help
thinking
that when she
said *Let her do*
what she needs
to do she was
on some level
talking
about
herself.

Eventually
my dog loses
interest in the
woman, or I pull
her away, or I throw
a treat a little distance
down the sidewalk,
I don't remember
how that part
unfolds, but I
do remember the
woman crossing
the street, climbing
into her vehicle,
a Jeep, not a soccer
mom SUV (I hate the
term "soccer mom" for
all of its condescension,
its coded
misogyny, I hate

that "soccer mom" is
where my mind
has gone)
but a
Jeep Jeep, the kind
I longed for
as a teenager in
West Virginia—
brown queer closeted
(did
I long for the Jeeps
or for the boys who
drove them?)—a
Jeep with big wheels
& thick tread
& manual gears,
a Jeep that could
cross creeks,
climb mountains,
that could tear
down a dirt road
no matter mud
or obstacle
or incline
or inclement
weather
& drive to the
very edge of the
wide river
that defines
our town
& where
gathered

teens—
so easy in their
bodies
& sense of
belonging &
of what belonged
to them—
swimming,
boating,
drinking, a
Jeep that could
take me all
those places I
wasn't allowed—&
never dared—to
go. And now I know
what I've always known
even if I don't
yet understand:
that the woman
with the lipstick the
color of crushed
cranberries when
she said
what she said
was also
talking
about
me.

PRACTICING

I went to school with your son, says the man who thinks he knew me but never knew me.

He says this to my father as he is prepping my father for surgery.

Bedside, he is where I would be were we not in the midst of a pandemic: no visitors in the hospital, no exceptions.

Even my mother has had to deposit my father curbside, like recycling, or raked leaves.

About this man who thinks he knew me but never knew me, I remember the following: that he was a soccer star, that he was casually cruel to me in the way that straight boys back then were, that in sixth grade on a class trip I found him rolling around in the motel bed with another popular boy and when I asked them what they were doing they replied—mincingly, meanly—*practicing!*

For years, *practicing!* sat in my stomach like the swallowed stone of a mealy peach.

For years I practiced being all kinds of things I had no business being. For years I practiced being everyone but me.

I hope this man who thinks he knew me but never knew me comforts my father, is gentle with him, speaks to him in a soft, calm voice, finds a way to remind him how deeply and completely he is loved, how even alone he is not alone.

I hope this man who thinks he knew me but never knew me proves to be a man I think I know but never knew.

GHAZAL

for my grandmother

You collected fallen petals from a rose
in West Virginia, clad in sari pink of rose.

You didn't have the English to ask permission from our neighbors.
Our neighbors' bush, our neighbors' fence, our neighbors' rose.

What had fallen on this side of the fence, you reasoned, was yours,
for your gods, fresh garlands, you'd sew of marigold and rose.

Your meticulous altar a reminder of your lost world;
your statues, your prayer beads, your deities in careful rows.

Did they tell the truth, wise Shakespeare and Stein, those years ago?
Would by any other name it smell as sweet? Is a rose a rose?

Or does it matter the language, the color, the country, the word?
Is there a there there? By the Arabian Sea: a rose.

How ashamed I was of you in white America.
To that mean, scared younger self, I offer a white rose.

Still, I shunned you, failed to hear through you my past.
Lost lessons, stories, scattered petals from a rose.

Years later, I'm aware my own trespasses, ever so slightly,
onto stoop or yard to steal the scent of a neighbor's rose.

Aware, as well, the dangers of trespassing while brown.
In "post-racial America" (ha!), my glasses are not tinted rose.

Your ghost whispers to me in a language I'm trying to learn.
To you I raise my glass—late May, rosé.

Trying to learn, too, from Rumi and Hafiz, the art of unforgetting.
I must answer for myself: What was lost? And what, Rahul, arose?

LOST & FOUND

The shawl I wear always & thought was my grandfather's I learned
recently is not.

I examine my hair from multiple angles with a hand
mirror & am horrified by what I see.

I am forty-seven; which is to say:
some things have happened & some have not.

The shawl I once lost on
a trail in Boulder, but, still believing it to be my grandfather's,
backtracked until I found it, which wasn't easy.

Almost everyone I tell
about my thinning hair admits they too have lost this past year.

I ask my
mother, *Are you sure?* and she says, *Yes, all your grandfather's things
were burned.*

We were not close. We were the opposite of close. Maybe
that is why I needed the shawl.

The shampoo & conditioner I bought
are not doing me any favors, but the big bottles were a better value &
there is still so much left.

Fire, I've been told, can cleanse.

I am trying
to decide—knowing what I now know—if it still keeps me warm.

EVERY POEM I WRITE IS CALLED "FEEDING THE GHOSTS" INCLUDING THIS ONE

In my head I'm making a terrible pun about the insects swarming our dining room table: *antcestors*. Also on the table: a Día de los Muertos candle molded in pale yellow beeswax, wilting white roses, a small cream-colored ceramic silo with a gold leaf slit thrown and fired by a friend that she calls a "spirit house," a tarot card stamped with a skull, and a collection of cup-shaped forest-gathered treasures—broken nutshells, curled leaves, warped wet bark. We know these last items are likely the source of the ants, but Robert half-jokes, half-not that they must live in the spirit house, though neither of us has seen them go in or out. It is true: I have, of late, been calling on the ancestors, designating empty chairs for them, offering them tangerines in bone china teacups splurge-purchased in Delhi a decade ago, delicate edges etched with red and gold roses. I've made offerings, also, to the antcestors: dinner crumbs I do not brush from the marigold tablecloth, scraps of a late-night sandwich left on a plate until morning. But the antcestors overwhelm me, and, days later, I return the forest-gathered items to their rightful place and carry the antcestors onto the fire escape with file folders. I'd like to think I do not harm them, not a single one, but I know it's not true. The antcestors are fragile and I am clumsy, as all humans are, and easily distracted, and my thumbs, after all, are anvils, are cannonballs, are cyclones spun by a warming planet, are avalanches, are hammers more accustomed to pounding out smart phone missives than ushering into the next world—or gently across this one—tiny visiting souls.

COPPER BEECH

The innkeeper told me about the tree out back, how its leaves in fall drop all at once. *It's magic,* he said. *One day full and golden, then suddenly bare.*

But I was distracted, still thinking about the ghosts who greeted me in the entryway—one with breath like lilacs but with the ragged edge of rot, another whose hair, in the air, ignited wild, swirling currents.

They have joined me now as I sit prim in the parlor sipping cream sherry from a thin-stemmed glass, imagining I am someone else, not a middle-aged, Indian American writer struggling to make ends meet, but rather Maggie Smith in *Downton Abbey* or some similarly privileged and tragic English dame.

The literature on the cocktail table says there is a likelihood—though not a certainty—that this rural Pennsylvanian house was once a stop on the Underground Railroad. I am a visitor now, but I once lived in these parts, or close enough, and I experienced enough to question whether anyone here helps anyone who doesn't look like them. But I try to stuff my bitterness into my pockets, along with a purloined biscuit for later because I like something sweet before bed, and extras for the ghosts should I need to feed them.

The literature on the cocktail table also promises a dog, but I see none, and the next morning when I ask the wife of the man who told me about the tree, her face will fall and she will say, *That dog is dead*, and I will immediately think, *Buried beneath the copper beech*, but I will know enough not to ask.

I am here to visit an Asian American literature class at the college in town to discuss my short story about trying to find a way to love a grandfather I thought I couldn't, a short story that took me a year to write and then two or three years to let sit and then another year to rewrite and another to gather my courage to send out, all more than a decade ago. The story is autobiographical but fictionalized, and I have long forgotten what is true.

Tonight I will have dinner with a Vietnamese American literature professor who was once a lawyer, a Vietnamese American drag queen and visual artist who was also once a lawyer, and a Cambodian American poet. We will talk about immigrant parents, refugee parents, the Khmer Rouge, a long and cruel American war, lost relatives, dead relatives, murdered relatives, reeducation camps, boats piled with people in impossibly dark nights, racism and homophobia in West Virginia and in central Pennsylvania and in western New York and in eastern Pennsylvania, generational trauma and generational silences. We will talk about how to tell painful stories that need to be told and about how, too, to tell stories of joy—immigrant joy, brown joy, femme joy, queer joy—and about how hard this is.

How hard this is.

What if you miss it? I asked the man. *The magic day?* He shrugged. *That tree's been there a hundred years. There'll be other falls.*

But now I want to see it, the tree when it releases, all at once, all it has been holding. I want to know what kind of wind it takes. Or maybe it takes no wind at all. Maybe when the time is right it takes only will and the cellular wisdom for the tree to know it needs to let go to let grow something new.

III.

THE PROMOTION

If I get
the promotion
maybe we will buy
a house, one of those
old mill worker houses
in Germantown
from the 1800s.
We will
paint the trim
purple & we'll
plant a garden
& tend
to the ghosts
who live
in the house,
even though
I am terrified of ghosts
& I don't
particularly love
old houses,
at least
not the way
some people
love old houses.
But I also
don't love

new houses
& an old house
is the kind
we can afford
if I get
the promotion.
If I don't get
the promotion
perhaps we will stay
where we are
in this apartment,
which, it's true,
has its problems.
But,
    Oh!
how I love
the century-old
sycamores
out front
who wave at us
through the fourth floor
windows,
& the slow
way
the sun
moves
from one end
of the apartment
to the other,
& the ghosts,
no, I don't love
the ghosts,
but we

have gotten
used to
each other
& have
long ago
made our
peace.

LONGBOAT KEY

was it a lifetime ago that i set the sun

flowers in the warm gulf waters,

golden explosions not garden-grown

but publix-bought though any pot

or plot of soil tended is as sacred

as the next? the water was the blue

of childhood, the setting sun

bubblegum, the floating flowers

a ceremony revealing itself

in real time.

in the publix parking lot

when i bought the sunflowers along

with oranges and soft cheese, a man

approached me, sir, he said,

sir, please, my son is in the hospital,

i need money for gas, it's urgent,

i'm not lying, see? and he tried to show

me his cell phone, but i said, sir, i am

sorry for your son, i believe you,

you do not have to prove to me

anything, and i gave him a twenty.

i juiced the oranges and ate the cheese

and swam in the gulf and dug

digits into dazzling sand

and for three days gazed at the sun

flowers in a plastic pitcher

by the picture window

and thought about

the past and the future

and what i wanted and what

i thought i needed and what life

was likely to grant me and what

i would have to fight for.

but it isn't true, the story i've told

about the man in the parking lot.

i did not call him sir, i did not say

i believe you. i let him show

me—and i could smell him

when he did this, sharp and

sour and full of need—the smudged

44

screen of his scratched and dented

flip phone, the text in all caps that

could have been from anyone

that said only HELP.

in the water the flowers

did not dance the way i

thought they would. the ocean,

a salsa dancer said, is polyrhythmic.

currents above and currents below.

something is always happening

you cannot see.

TUNNELS

1.

The women sitting behind me on the commuter train cycle through conversation topics: the stable where they both keep horses, their children who attend the same Waldorf school, the Paris vacation one of them took last fall, the rain that fell and all but ruined it. The women are white and boarded the train in one of Philadelphia's wealthiest neighborhoods. I note both of these facts, even as I chide myself for doing so. Irritated by their privilege—irritated by my own irritation—I am already directing unkind thoughts their way when their conversation turns to—their voices dropping to a whisper—the tunnels.

"Colorful" is how one of them describes them, the underground pedestrian corridors that connect the subway stations in Center City and run for several blocks beneath Broad Street, tunnels the women resort to walking through—as do I—when the weather is too harsh to walk aboveground, tunnels I am guessing we will walk through this morning given the whipping winds, the freezing rain. I have seen what they have seen: the extensive unhoused population that seeks shelter down there—folks with their belongings in bags or carts, sitting or lying on cardboard; bodies wrapped in dirty blankets or buried in sleeping bags; mostly men, mostly people of color, sometimes women, on rare occasions children; folks dealing drugs; folks buying drugs; folks doing drugs; once, a circle of six or seven people passing a needle. I have also seen a woman combing her daughter's hair, humming; a man reading a beat-up Tom Clancy paperback; a man listening to the news on a portable radio and cuddling with a pit bull; a man unfolding, shaking out, and refolding his clothes, placing them carefully into a soiled duffel bag.

It's awful, one woman says. *Sometimes you don't want to see that. It's been a long day. You just want to go home.*

I don't know whether to feel sad or angry, the other woman says. *They could change their lives if they wanted to. It's not easy, but they could change. Not all of them, but most of them.*

It's awful.

It's sad.

They sigh, and then, their voices returning to normal volume, they move on to the next topic: the online clothing concierge website they both subscribe to.

My stylist is terrible. She keeps sending me loud prints. Do I look like a loud person?

That's not you at all.

2.

There is a moment, a moment that I have perhaps misinter-preted, a moment that maybe means something different than what I think it means, a moment when we have gotten off the train and we are walking through the station, into the tunnels, and I am walking through a doorway and the women are just behind me and my tote bag gets caught on the door. I am stuck and I have to turn around to get my bag unhooked and there they are. We are face-to-face, and the women look—and maybe this is the part I am misinterpreting, assigning meaning that isn't there—the women look, what? surprised? irritated? scared? to be face-to-face with a brown, male-presenting figure they do not know and who has stopped and turned around in a doorway for reasons that maybe aren't readily apparent to them. I don't know if they are thinking any of these things. What I do know is that they do not smile, even when they realize—if they hadn't already realized—why I have stopped in the first place.

3.

Maybe I'm wrong. In spite of my gender presentation, my skin color, it's hard for me to imagine anyone feeling threatened by me. After all, the tote bag that got caught on the door is one that I sewed myself and has shimmering gold peacocks on the outside and, for the lining, hot pink fabric dotted with cartoon skulls.

Do I look like a loud person?

That's not you at all.

But it is impossible to know what people might feel threatened by. It is impossible to know what people wish they didn't have to see.

4.

Later that day—despite the whipping winds, the freezing rain—I shuttle aboveground between department stores in search of a new winter coat. I find one I love. It fits perfectly. Is $250 too much to pay for a parka if it's replacing a jacket I bought eighteen years earlier?

I look again in the fitting-room mirror. I see a person who is stylish, self-assured. The faux-fur trim on the hood frames their face, makes their eyes look brighter, makes their skin glow. It's me, but better.

For much of the past six years, working as an adjunct college creative writing teacher, I have been hovering not far above the federal poverty level. This is based on income, although I know that income is only part of the story when it comes to true poverty. I have resources many in my income bracket do not, including generous, financially-comfortable family members whom I can ask for money should I need it, who routinely offer me money even when I don't ask.

Recently, my fortunes have changed, and I feel flush for the first time in years. I have a full-time teaching job and, at the moment, my salary is perhaps 30 percent higher than it's ever been in my twenty-plus years of adulthood, although it is still probably less than a tenth of the household income of the women on the train. Still, I am more like them than I am like the folks in the tunnels. For now.

On the way to the register, caressing the luxurious trim on the hood, I think to check the label and realize that the faux fur is real fur, fox fur. I return it to the rack.

5.

I am embarrassed by how much I enjoy wandering through the cavernous department store, sliding across the shiny tiled floors, gazing up at the gold chandeliers. I stop to contemplate a cashmere throw. I am ashamed by how much I enjoy the deferential way the sales clerk asks me how he may help.

6.

As a small child, I was terrified of tunnels of any sort. When my family took road trips and we had to pass through one, my parents would go to great lengths to distract me so I wouldn't scream and cry. I don't know what frightened me so much, but I'm guessing it was the darkness, how everything that had been there—the sky, the trees, the great world around me—was suddenly gone.

Now I marvel at the structures as feats of engineering, the way they burrow through hard earth, through mountains, underneath rivers—the way they bridge distances, connect people and places that are close but far away.

7.

The next day, I will be walking through the woods—woods in which I twice have had what I would describe as a spiritual experience with a fox. The weather will still be gray, even if the whipping winds and freezing rain are gone. I will be tapping out this essay on my phone while walking, and there will be a break in the clouds, and the flecks of mica sparkling in the stone and in the dirt will dazzle my attention away from my screen. And for a moment, for better or for worse, the women on the train and the folks in the tunnels and the department store with its shiny tiled floors and the parka that was me but better will all vanish, and this moment will be the only moment: the sparkling mica, the silvery creek below, the birds I cannot see but can hear, though I haven't learned their calls. I will finish writing this piece weeks later, one afternoon after teaching, sitting in a café in Center City; in front of me, beside my computer, a four-dollar cappuccino and a honey-gold canelé on a black porcelain dish; waiting to order at the register, a man in loafers holding a chihuahua in a Louis Vuitton dog carrier, two more Chihuahuas at his feet on narrow leather leashes and in houndstooth sweaters; on a wooden bench next to the door, a disheveled, seemingly unhoused man I have seen here before, trying to get warm. Below us: tunnels.

UPON ENCOUNTERING A DESI FRIEND AT A WRITING CONFERENCE

She asked if I had an extra bindi,
and I said, *No, just the one I'm wearing.*

Later, I understood I should have stashed
in my bag or pocket a packet of extras

for just such a friend, or in case
mine fell off (which it did

while I was talking to a poet I knew
not well and hadn't seen

in years, the bling fluttering confetti-like,
the poet, without comment, bending

to retrieve it), but I wasn't raised a girl,
wasn't taught such things, was taught

other things. Should I have peeled
for her from my own brow that tear-

shaped and sacred mark? But, oh!
how I needed that day this third

eye for clarity and protection. How I needed
to know there were forces at work

I couldn't yet see, that some new way
was blinking open.

FOUR SLIPS

The first slip
I offered
the colonizer
was *robert*
but she looked
at me
askance
& Robert
to my right
said, *Really?!*
never mind
I appeared nowhere
on any of
his four slips
of what he
cherished most
& it was just
a decolonizing-
the-classroom
exercise besides.
So I gave her
instead
ritualceremonyprayer.

*

The next time
the colonizer
didn't ask.
She hovered,
surveying
my three
remaining
slips,
her breath hot,
her yellow hair
like lightning,
then flicked away
two more—
robert then *dog*.

*

I no longer
remember
what was on
the slip
she allowed
me to keep—
beauty?
hope?

the towering sycamore
whose leaves in summer
hum me to sleep?
I must
have known
even then
the fire
that was
to come.

AT THE WORKPLACE MEETING ON DIVERSITY EQUITY & INCLUSION

the senior
administrator
said,
let me
address
the elephant
in the
room. . .

but then
he didn't
and addressed,
instead,
the centipede
scurrying
along
the floor
searching
for safety,

one hundred
legs
never
enough
to escape
the senior
administrator's
tasseled
loafer
hovering
perpetually
mid-
squish.

evening,
i tend
my altar,
offer
my four-
armed
elephant-
headed
god—
remover of
obstacles—
orange
segments
and peanuts.

i whisper,
Lord. . .

57

MORNING PRAYER

A December morning the color of underwear,
sleet pelting the rattling windows and thin roof.

I listen to Arooj Aftab and gaze at the blue bedroom wall.
Refuge the paint's called, and, in the hallway,

Agreeable Gray. It is the last day of the semester.
My students will present projects. I will recite

"Wild Geese" by Mary Oliver, as I always do,
and I'll try to say the right words in the right

order, will try not to let my voice tremble when I speak
the opening line about not needing to be good.

Yesterday, in a faculty meeting, a white professor
said I should be ashamed I'd never read Dante, and I said,

I'm not. I said other things, too, things that were hard
for me to say, and the exchange, though civil, ate at me

for hours after. But that was yesterday, not today. Today,
I will pass the morning gazing at the blue wall,

the way one might gaze at the ocean, soothing
despite (or because of) its vastness and dark mystery.

I will take refuge in my small blue notebook,
and in waves crashing onshore,

the iterative way, both urgent and patient,
they write and rewrite the world.

SEEDS

My partner Robert and I are visiting my parents in West Virginia in the town where I grew up, just days after the white president of the United States told four congresswomen of color to go back to where they came from. It is summer and we are in my parents' air-conditioned sunroom marveling at the twenty or more birds clustered around my mother's backyard bird feeder. There are big birds and tiny birds and even a rogue squirrel and a chipmunk, and at some point my mother fetches her iPad and pulls up a field guide to local birds. We do our best to name what we see, but this has never been my strength.

Sunflower seeds, my mother says. *That's the secret. They go crazy for sunflower seeds. It's all about the seeds.*

Yesterday my mother hovered and grumbled and chortled and sighed as I tried to teach myself to make dal from a recipe in *Indian-ish*. I knew she was irritated that I wasn't asking her for her dal recipe, instead turning to this cookbook written by a second-generation Indian American who writes about learning to cook from her own mother and grandmother. When I asked for ghee, my mother said she has never used ghee; a little canola oil is just fine. When I asked for fresh lime, she handed me a plastic bottle from the fridge. When I asked her for a strainer to drain the water, she said, *Use your fingers—you are Indian, that's how Indians do it,* and I said, *I am Indian-ish,* but I used my fingers anyway. Despite the substitutions, the dal, I thought, turned out delicious, but she called the dal something in Gujarati and then said in English, *This is what babies eat.*

The next day, my mother tells me she and her Indian women friends laughed about it when they went for their walk that morning. I don't tell her that the park where they walk is—as I discovered the summer I came home from my first year in college—a cruising spot for gay sex.

The sunroom is part of an elaborate three-tier deck with a swing on the middle tier that my mother loves because it reminds her of her childhood in India, the jhulas in everyone's houses and courtyards, cold glasses of nimbu pani, crows on the windowsills.

The day Robert and I depart West Virginia to drive back to Philadelphia, we read in the local paper that the KKK has marched through a nearby town. They left behind—all over the town and on folks' doorsteps—white supremacist pamphlets affixed to small bags of birdseed. Interviewed, a local official said it wasn't a hate crime issue, it was a littering issue.

Later, as I am trying to merge onto the highway exit, a car pulls up beside me and a white man in his twenties leans out of the passenger side window and makes a gesture. Robert tells me it is a common white supremacist sign, but I don't believe him until

I look it up much later. Still, I am rattled enough that I take the wrong exit ramp and end up traveling south instead of north and have to turn around at the next exit, which is some miles away.

Days later I am jogging in my Philadelphia neighborhood and white teenagers in a passing car shout something at me and I can't make out the words, but their tone and the looks on their faces are clear and I wonder: Is it because I am brown or is it because I am gay (do I jog gay?) or is it because they don't like the team on my ballcap (Go Heels!) and are they going to circle back and follow me home?

I make that dal from *Indian-ish* all the time. I use ghee and fresh limes and a strainer, not my fingers, but the spices come from a stainless steel masala dabba my mother gave me and I always think of her when I eat it, always think this is my mother's dal, even though it is not.

About the backyard birdfeeder: what astonished and gladdened us was how many, and of what variety, were being fed.

About the littering: I want to know what they do with those seeds.

IV.

AFTER A POEM BY JAMES WRIGHT

i have wasted my life,
i wake
thinking
this morning,
most mornings.
and yet,
outside
my bedroom
birds
are whistling
their millennia-old
song
& the sun-smacked
window
in the front
room
where the dog
sleeps
is the shimmering
rectangular pendant
of the gold

necklace
my mother
bought me
in little india
when i was thirteen—
om on one side,
laxmi and ganesh
on the other—
a precious item
promptly placed
in a safe-deposit box
& which i didn't
see again—
except
on special
occasions—
for nine years,
when i,
my parents said,
was finally
a responsible

adult.
i wore it
off and on
for two decades,
but now
it has been
sitting
some six
years
cleft
in a turkish
box
from my ex-
sister-in-law,
awaiting
whatever
small
effort
from me
to make it
again whole.

MORNING PRAYER

Salem, Connecticut

Was the winged creature
outside my window,
backlit by morning light
and silhouetted through the

sheer curtain, a butterfly
or a hummingbird? Heavy
in my bed, I want to learn
its lesson of flight

and fancy, of landing
lightly, of allowing
the wind to carry me
where I want to go.

O that my nightmares,
having condensed like dew,
evaporate now
in summer sunlight.

O that we all
experience, at least for
a moment, this dis-
appearance into air.

WHY WE WOKE TOO EARLY

Because one of us had to pee and the other, having been disturbed, checked their phone, only wanting to see the time, but somehow ended up in their email. Because we are both stressed out about different things, though it is always the same thing. Because the curtain in the bedroom is a pink sari draped over a metal rod and one of us didn't close it properly the night before and the pre-dawn glow was already seeping around its edges and it is too sheer to keep out much light anyway and the sari in that ghostly light reminded one of us of their dead grandmother. Because our dog, lying in her bed in the curtainless living room, was sending us telepathic messages that she was already awake and hungry and needed our reassurance, as she does every morning, that we haven't vanished. Because we went to bed too late and drank too much wine or maybe not enough wine or maybe what we should have been drinking was scotch or chamomile tea or warm milk or water from the pitcher on the kitchen counter poured into matching artist-made cups with patterns that are leaves but always look to one of us like flames. Because we've needed a new mattress for at least three years. Because we have a ceiling fan above our bed and as any feng shui practitioner will tell you that is a capital N, capital O NO-NO (but oh! how nice it feels in August when it's whirring on high and we are lying naked on top of sweat-soaked sheets). Because when one of us checked the time on their phone and ended up in their email they saw that they hadn't gotten a job they didn't really want and had applied to reluctantly and mostly out of fear and yet somehow the not getting the job made them wonder if they had, in their life, done everything wrong. Because the world was calling to us—the world is always calling to us!—but this morning we were paying attention to the wrong voices. Because one of us needed to write this and to read it out loud—the catch of regret in their voice; outside, snowflakes settling on the iron fire escape—while the other—standing over a pot of bubbling oatmeal, stirring—listened.

MORNING PRAYER

August, and Kimona is watching me from the corner of the bedroom, waiting for me to stir. Robert has been up for an hour or more, rattling around in the kitchen, doing whatever it is morning people do. Kimona wants someone to open the door so she can join him, begin her day, but she is a good dog, or rather, she is a bad dog who is trying to be good, and so she doesn't want to wake me. But then it happens: I sigh and turn, and there she is, standing suddenly at the side of the bed, her tail like a pinwheel spinning faster and faster. The heavy curtains and rumbling window unit have kept our bedroom dark and cool, so I am not quite ready for the assault of heat and light when I swing open the door, and—as with so many days of late—I am not sure I can face this one. After letting her out, I climb back into bed and hermetically reseal the room.

Yesterday evening Robert and I played tennis. Swatting the ball, I remembered childhood. I wrote in my journal, *I had a happy childhood* and then thought better of it and added *aside from the racism*, and then, *aside from the racism and homophobia*, and then, *aside from the racism and homophobia and xenophobia*. But it is true: I had a happy childhood. I was a happy child. Everyone says so.

In the dark bedroom I try to recall last night's dreams, scanning them for messages. I start constructing in my head a gratitude list. I think about the cold cantaloupe already cut up in the fridge and how good it will taste. I think about the book I've been reading which I like but do not love. I try not to think about the unanswered emails in my inbox. I try not to think about the news or the weeks and months of uncertainty gathering like rainwater in an ever-deepening pool, the impossible task of trying to swim through it. Two hours pass. Maybe three. I have not moved.

The bedroom door squeaks open. Robert is bringing me coffee. And behind him, Kimona, who has already done everything, has had her breakfast and her walk, has chased a hare and dug a hole and grazed on grass and played with Satchel and splashed in the kiddie pool Josh sets out in summer. She trots in, happy and proud, carrying in her mouth neither a ball nor her favorite squeaky cupcake, but the sun, the earth, the air, the whole bright world, filthy and gleaming and wild and redolent. She lays it at the foot of the bed, lies down next to it. She is a good dog. Or rather, she is a bad dog trying to be good. I am trying too. I am trying in every way I know how. She will wait.

MORNING PRAYER

Seeing a squirrel this morning
in the September sun—
shadows & light
lacing the lawn—
laboring over a huge apple,
Jupiter-bright, scarcely carriable
up the steep tree,
my heart swells for
the ways in which
we are all trying our best to survive,
to seize when we can some
sunshine.
What scavenged
incandescence have I squirreled
away for tonight?
In the dark halls
of the house that is Big Me,
Little Me keeps stumbling,
stubbing their toe,
crying out.
Do they remember
they have filled their cupboards
with the patter of rain
on new leaves,
with river rocks, mica-flecked, shimmering
like ankle bells in a Bharatanatyam
dance?

THE GATHERING

Fuck that shit,
says my wisest friend

about the journal prompt
demanding

three things
I'm excited for

today. I can name
none, never could, can

count on one hand
the mornings I've woken

bright-eyed & ready.
A thousand mornings

of dread, I say instead,
which accounts

for not quite three years
but by which I mean

my whole life.
So what? says the friend.

Maybe it takes
a thousand mornings

of dread to bring about
the gathering

by which she means
the poems

I've written
in the dark.

What else
have I gathered?

Not shattered pieces.
I don't want them

& have given them
to the creek.

Robert gathers garden
vegetables & other

things that feed us.
Our dog gathers

toys in her bed.
Maybe it's not

what we've gathered
but rather what gathers.

Mist, for instance, that
moonlit night. Wind.

Swifts in the chimney
of the pandemic-shuttered school.

Or stars in the sky,
which seemed last night

(is it possible?)
so much closer.

MORNING PRAYER

I had wanted only
a few moments of peace
when I sat
this morning
on the iron fire escape,
coffee in a yellow cup,
a single sunflower in a
squat glass vase
on the small breakfast table,
not knowing somewhere unseen
a lawn mower
was about to roar.
Life's been
like this: nothing
quite right, disruptions
everywhere.
Yesterday,
the rain we thought
would blow over instead
persisted,
dampening our precious
long-planned beach day.
That morning,
standing at the sink,
referencing personal struggles,
I told Robert—borrowing something

I heard a friend say—*I trust
my ability to repair,* and just
then the thunder clapped—
clapped or clapped back?—so loud
the apartment shook
and the cells in my body
hid for hours under their
desks. Still, that afternoon
we swam in the gray
Atlantic, dark clouds above
and rain falling, the two
of us taking turns
racing into the
mighty waves where we
felt not threatened,
but held. Listening now
to the lawnmower, I am
remembering
mornings meditating
at an ashram near
Neyyar Dam, and the lions'
roars from across
the lake. For days,
buying into the most
cliché tropes about
"exotic India," I believed
the lions roamed wild
in the jungle,
only to learn
it was a preserve and our
morning meditation happened
to coincide with
feeding time; their

roar was one of hunger.
The sunflower—
itself lionlike—
I had cut and rearranged
because its heavy
head kept causing
a taller, more delicate
vase to topple.
As I finish my coffee,
I realize
I am hungry.
I am hungry still.

Q & A

Do you want the sun at your back or on
your face?

I want the sun everywhere, in every crevice
& cell, a trillion tiny suns, shrunk but potent,
dissolving in my bloodstream like Kool-Aid
crystals, no, Tang!—the drink of astronauts,
of space walks, of the moon and Mars, of
galaxies far, far away.

You do know Mars is the god of war, right?

In my blood I want, too, a trillion Maha
Kalis spinning like the Tasmanian Devil
cartoon, their tongues & sharp blades
obliterating all that does not belong inside
me, each severed head on their trillion tiny
necklaces rising & setting & rising into
eternity.

Who do you love more, the sun or the moon?

I asked my dog this. She did what she does
when she doesn't know what to do: bent her
front paws, showed me her tummy & waited
for the necessary.

Will you be able to sleep tonight?

With moonlight as my blanket? Yes. With
the sun in my veins? Yes. With the trillion
spinning Maha Kalis, the trillion spinning
suns, the trillion spinning earths, the one I
can see and the nine hundred ninety-nine
billion nine hundred ninety-nine million
nine hundred ninety-nine thousand nine
hundred-ninety nine I cannot? Yes! Oh,
yes. Yes!

V.

THE POND GLITTERING

in the distance
    this bright morning
        is every water

        I've ever known
    is the mud-colored
Little Kanawha
of my childhood

feline against
    my small town's legs,
        purring, *Follow me*
          into the Ohio

        into the Mississippi
    into the Gulf
into the Atlantic,
purring, *You are*

not alone,
    is high in the
        Himalayas
          Ganga Ma as she

tightens her sari
& begins her slow
descent into the
plains into the

clamoring wailing
world, whispering,
Shh, it's okay,
I'm here, is the

Carolina quarry
into which I dove
that moonless night
not knowing but trusting

there was water below
enough to save me,
is the Schuylkill
is Turtle River

is Foster Lake
is the Wissahickon
is the Sabarmati
is the water

in my own body
again & again
swimming me back
to myself

          you are the dew
        on the grass
      you are the mist
in the valley

you are the drop
      in the spider's web
          in the eaves
                of the roof

                on the porch
          in the sun
        inside of which
shimmers the entire

              world

THREE OF CUPS

i love
where waters
meet

1.
point park,
parkersburg,
west virginia,
or, anyrivertown,
u.s.a.

2.
kanniyakumari
where the tip
of india's
tongue, sharp
as kali's—
& aflame—
licks three
shimmering
bodies

3.
in the woods
i walk
weekly,
the clear stream
trickling over
moss-splotched rocks
joining gently
cresheim creek

can i color
myself closer
to you? i heard
a dancer ask

water always
says
yes.

RACE POINT

i am a lover
of water
of bodies
of water
there isn't
a body
i do not
love
i do not
wish
to insert
my body
into
i am a lover
of things
worn
by water
by air
& sun & earth
too
canyons
sea glass
pebbles
driftwood
smooth

& faded as
an old
shirt
i am a lover
of things
worn & worn
a khadi kurta
purchased
20 yrs ago
in ahmedabad
so much me
it is second-skin
i am a lover
of things
worn & worn
my body
i am trying
to love
worn & worn
the ocean
worn & worn
& because
i do not understand
anything
of this world

i do not know
how the ocean
could be three feet
from my body
then two feet
from my body
then inches
from my body
then upon my body
the stones
drying
on my towel
are still beautiful
but everything
is more beautiful
in water
i am not
the first person
to write a poem
at race point
yesterday
i heard a writer
read a poem
written at race point
which is maybe

why i am
writing a poem
at race point
if you can call this
a poem
if you can call this
writing
if you can say
i am
writing
this poem
this poem
is writing
me
the water
is writing
earth
hundreds of miles
south
at this very
moment
a hurricane
bears down
the water
is writing

a new chapter
in which characters
minor & major
we have come to know
& love die
& because
i do not understand
anything of this
world
& because
i want to be
at the edge
where this
becomes that
i do not
have sense
to move my
towel
feet
i move it
inches
as the tide
rises
as the water
chases

me
i must move
again & again
until i
decide to
allow
this body
to become
that body
allow the water
in this body
to become the water
in that body
allow that
body to write
this body
allow these bodies
to do what
all bodies
always
long
to do

THE BIRDS

1.

Salem, Connecticut
Is the fat bird pecking
in the spring grass injured?
For an hour she's hopped

not more than a few feet,
tipping her beak dirtward
between gazing at me.

Fly, robin, fly, I want
to sing, *so I know you
can.* But I don't & she

doesn't. Meanwhile, evening
is brushing dusk across
the valley, stroke by stroke.

Tonight, we will tend our
wounds, whatever they be.

2.

Salem, Connecticut
The woodpecker tells me now is not the time
to do whatever it is I think I am doing

at this small desk in a Connecticut cabin
this June afternoon. He says, *Listen*

to me whoop and gurgle, listen closely
so that next time you might find a more precise
word than gurgle; *listen to me hop &*
tap & scratch & scramble as I re-

position myself on this tree. He says,
Learn the name of this tree—for earth's sake—&
of the one over there; hear the color my crown
paints the air (crimson clatter), & once I've

flown: listen, keep listening. He says,
                                        This
is the poem.

3.

Philadelphia
In an oblong puddle abutting the train tracks,
a bathing robin chases away a small sparrow.

I briefly worry, but it has rained plenty & the sorrow
easily finds another silty pool in which to wallow.

Did I say sorrow? I meant sparrow.
Did I say wallow? I meant swallow,

not the bird swallow, the verb swallow,
swallowed, will swallow, as in, I will swallow what I am given,

I will wallow in whatever dip or groove or hole
will accept my body & make me whole, make me know

I am of—& wanted by—this filthy & precious earth.

THREE THINGS I AM
GRATEFUL FOR TODAY

Does it have to be
today, things peculiar
to *today*, or can they
be the same as
yesterday, or the
day before or before or
before?—my gratitude
is deep but circumscribed,
like a well, like a dark
hole—and why three?
why always three? the
world loves three:
the Father the Son the Holy Ghost,
Brahma Vishnu Shiva,
Kelly Michelle Beyoncé,
no room for LaTavia,
never room for LeToya.
So here it is,
what I am grateful
for today:
the eggs
in the nest
in the eaves
of the train station,

eggs I cannot
count for the
brooding bird
who does not leave,
not for the rumble
of trains
or human heads
that stream beneath
every hour or so
or teens
toking
on the bench
at midnight
or me & my dog—
monsters both—
the bird does not fly
does not flinch
does not move,
this bird sits & waits.
And now I am
realizing I am
not grateful for
the eggs,
I am grateful for
the bird,
this brooding bird,
& for the birds—
one two three,
mother father brother—
who brooded
over
me.

VI.

SYCAMORE

Is it because I didn't fight hard enough
to save you, didn't anticipate that
on the other side of these losses were

more? On the block, two tall sycamores
were cut down quick, but you, gentle
third, stood another thirty-six days.

Is it wrong to say the men
in the branches that winter day were
beautiful? The men who hurt us

often are. We hugged each other
every night until they returned.
Now these many months later—

our losses like rings on our
brown heart stumps—I remember
barely what it was to behold

you and to be held.

LAST YEAR

I wore my glitter boots to the gathering—
New Year's Eve 2019—forgetting
I'd be removing them before entering. I didn't know
this would be a metaphor for the year to come.
What else did I leave at the door?
Will it all still be waiting for me when it's over &
will I still want it?
There are benefits to being barefoot—feeling
the ground beneath me, for one—& luckily
I wore cute socks striped in a purple not too purple
& a gray not too gray. I always wear striped socks
with those sparkly boots, thinking of the Wicked Witch
of the East. Don't get me wrong:
I have no intention of being crushed by a house,
but one never knows what will fall
from the sky & I want to be prepared, want
my protruding limbs, given the worst, to look
sickening. I'm muddying metaphors, I know, but muddy
is what I've got & I'm slowly learning to let things be
what they are, where they are, where
I left them.

APRIL 27TH, 2020

My timeline is full of dead men.

An Instagram account I follow has, for some weeks, been posting
panels of the AIDS Memorial Quilt. The men are all beautiful.
Their panels are adorned with flamingoes, musical instruments,
muscle cars. In one, a teddy bear wearing a cowboy hat and a
Lone Star State bandana spells out the dead man's name with a
lasso. In another, stylized tulips throw their heads back in joy.

Today is my birthday.

*

Yesterday, beneath the weeping cherry outside my building,
the Gold Star Family again left their annual memorial for their
dead son/brother/uncle/lover/friend/&c/&c/&c. . . , born the
same year as I was: a plaque, three American flags, cut flowers
in a plastic cup.

*

Last week, I told my students that a core tenet of Buddhism is
accepting the inevitability of one's own death, that learning how
to die teaches us how to live. We were discussing *Lincoln in the
Bardo*, so it seemed relevant. I'm not sure they agreed.

Maybe they didn't want to think about their deaths. I understood. Maybe I didn't want to think about mine.

*

Often the weeping cherry tree is in full bloom on my birthday, which is the soldier's death day. This must be why the Gold Star Family chose this species to plant in his honor. I have photos of myself on birthdays past standing beneath it, holding a bouquet of store-bought flowers, a cascade of pink falling around me (the soldier's memorial plaque floating somewhere out of the frame).

But this year is different. Today the blossoms are well past peak.

Next year, I will remember to notice them when they show themselves to me, whatever day that might be. I will take a moment to cherish them and thank them for their splendor. I will wish them well on their journeys as they flutter away on the breeze.

PEONIES

today is the last day
the store-bought peonies—
my birthday peonies!—
will be beautiful.
by evening, they will
have shed
their petals.
this morning
i rearranged them,
cut the stems
too short, put them
in the wrong vase,
but what's done
is done.
in my dream,
the cells in my body
were also rearranging—
it was painful.
it is painful still.
yesterday, the winds
and swirling rains were fierce.
during virtual class, a tree fell on
a student's barn and she
had to leave
our video call.
today is calm

and bright,
but when i open the
windows i can smell
the wet earth
and i know
there is more to come.

ONLY ONE

of the dozen
buds
will bloom;
I have come
to accept
this. This
one blossom—
pale & fragrant
& delicate
& ghostly—
is enough,
is more than
enough. In the
dark night
one need
only one
bright
moon.

LILIES

Overnight,
in the glass bottle
on the windowsill
on a single stalk
cut from a neighbor's yard
more than a week ago,
a second lily
has opened unexpectedly,
now two blossoms
splayed like ballerinas
or better yet
femme queens
fanning fingers
around their faces.
Flowers bloom: I don't know
why this should come as a
surprise to me or seem like a
small miracle, but
it does, this second blossom,
a second chance
to see and smell
the blessing for what it is,
always was.
A third bud,
small and green,
threatens to remain clenched

and shrivel where it is.
But so little I know
of what miracles
morning brings,
or of the exquisite
song the moon might
sing to make
the lily
sigh.

CREPE MYRTLE

1.

the very day i first
note, with delight, that the crepe

myrtles are finally in full
bloom—pink & red &

a deep coral the color of
my mother's necklace

i'd always reach for
as a child whenever she wore it—

i happen across (in a lonely
corner of the library,

in a book by an author
i'd never heard of) a short

poem about crepe myrtles,
which, of course, despite

its brevity (just seven
lines) is also about

something else.
& while i know

layers are part of
the beauty of poems

i sometimes long
for things to be

just one thing. why
must the coral be

the color of my mother's
necklace or the shrub

a symbol for *x* or *y*?
shall i try again?

2.

this hot august day
the crepe myrtle is

only what it is,
which is to say:

it is everything.

THE MEADOW

When did I ride my bicycle?
When did I sit in the meadow
watching the tall grasses sway,
bluebirds nesting in the apple tree,
and, across the rise, in dappled
sunlight, a cat curled on a
tree stump? Was it last week
or last year? Or was it
1983 in that small town
in the green hills?

I wore my pink shirt of faded
khadi, the one brought from Delhi
a lifetime ago, and sunglasses
because I couldn't bear the
brightness of the world.

When did I fly
down the steep street
ringing my bell?

Today is cold.
My dog is on
the bed. She is dreaming
again, her legs
twitching, her paws and

one pointed ear aflutter.
A gust rattles the windows.
I am grateful for my
wool blanket, for my warm dog
breathing beside me. I am grateful
for my bicycle
in the basement, my
memory of the meadow,
my faith that it is all still
there for me, waiting.

WHEN THE FLOOD COMES

At first she was allowed only when one of us was sick. Or depressed. And then of course on Mondays.

But now that we are always sick and depressed and it is always Monday it means our dog is always on our couch, which we bought for design, not for comfort, and which barely accommodates the two of us, let alone this eighty-pound beast.

She is on the bed, too, but only metaphorically, not actually *on* the bed—she couldn't get up here with her bad hip. Besides, we just bought a new mattress and there is a zero point five percent chance we may return it and I know zero point five percent seems like a tiny percent, but I dare not list the things that have happened these past months that had less than a zero point five percent chance of happening.

A friend says when you don't let pets on the furniture you are only punishing yourself. This may be true, but punishing myself is my religion, and it is hard to unravel what has been stitched into your genes by your ancestors' trembling fingers.

Our next couch will be huge and cream-colored (never mind the risk of stains and the fact our shedding dog is black) and it will take up the entire room.

The three of us will make our home there and when the flood comes (as surely it will, as surely it already has), we will float together happily for as long as the water allows.

WHAT WE SHOULD

The pale flower in the blue bowl
is doing what it should: browning

at the edges, allowing
its delicate petals to crinkle & curl.

Everything is a ceremony.

I recall the gold trim
of my grandmother's muted sari,

the sound of swishing,
a diya, a ceremony.

The shadows on the wall tell
stories I've heard & told

& heard & told
but never remember.

Stories are ceremonies.

The crimson leaves that fell
last fall from the Japanese maple

press their essence
into the winter walkway.

I remember spring, the blaze
of tulips in the neighbors' yard

but I was still there & not yet
here so how could it be?

We need a ceremony.

The snow tonight falls quietly
(as it always does)

& will be gone by morning.
Sunrise: a ceremony.

Each creature, in our own voice, sings.

EVENING PRAYER

I am sitting on the balcony in the dark. I have just eaten a peach, but I did not taste it.

A raga like a river is nearing its end. The tabla, once a trickle, is now a great fall, and Hariprasad Chaurasia on bansuri flute, a flickering fish.

The moon is behind a cloud behind a pine. I haven't seen its face in days.

On the small table, the pit of the peach sits in a Corelle bowl from a set I selected from a factory store when my parents moved me into my first college dorm. I thought the pattern was so modern and colorful. I thought I was going to be someone else. That was thirty years ago.

And I am just realizing: on the balcony in flickering candlelight, the tablecloth is patterned with sunflowers and there are fresh sunflowers in a cerulean vase and the molded candle is stamped with sunflowers. Sunflowers times three. Does this mean something? I want it to mean something. I want something to mean something. I need right now for something to mean something.

In the distance, again tonight: fireworks. A friend forwarded me an article trying to explain the uptick in pyrotechnics this summer, but I didn't read it and wouldn't have believed it anyway.

I don't read articles.

Tomorrow the moon will describe for me the taste of the peach. Tomorrow the moon will tell me everything.

SUMMER SOLSTICE

i don't have
the right camera
or the corresponding skills
to capture the lily
in the window,
the light
that dances
in sequined slippers
down the long
tongue of each
pitched petal,
or the way the
blossom turned to me
this morning,
full-faced,
guileless, and
smiled.

and because
perhaps
i am glum
by nature
i am already
thinking about
how this
surely is the

last day,
that by tomorrow,
or maybe the next,
the lily
will've
wilted,
and i'll find,
scattered on the dusty
sill, sad as
streamers
the day after a party,
six papery petals.

it terrifies me
how ephemeral everything
is, even
as i know
there is in this
a lesson.

yesterday,
finishing a long stroll
at dusk,
robert and i stopped to watch
a thrashing butterfly
pinched in a robin's beak,

its frantic yellow wings
sucking up
the last light
of the longest day
of the year.

it's always dark
. before we're home.

VII.

BEFORE & AFTER

My dream is full of violence.
I can't remember the details but

wake knowing what I already knew: I am not safe.

Seeing my dog, I sense she was there.
Does she remember? Did the same visions

visit her, curled in the corner, paws aflutter?

"What do you remember about the earth?" asks
Bhanu Kapil in a Jean Valentine poem.

I remember red rocks & rising sun.

I remember wildflowers in a mountain meadow,
cows with bells. To Kapil's question "How

will you/have you prepare(d) for your death?"

Valentine answers: "I know you brokenheart before this world,
and I know you after."

I remember cut grass.

I remember winged seeds & waterfalls,
everything finding its way.

UNDERWATER

On the trail, an old man with a red jacket & a blue backpack & trekking poles steams by in the opposite direction.

I say *old* but he is perhaps not so old, not so much older than I, I feel old, am old, am becoming old, have become this year so much older.

If I told you what hurts we would be here all day.

My dog does not like the old man or she does not like the trekking poles or she does not like his steam & so she growls & lunges as he passes.

She too is old, gray around the eyes & muzzle & the lip of her ear, her bad hip bothering her in ways I can only imagine.

The trees in the woods creak in the wind. The week has been wild. Today it may snow.

Far away, someone I dearly love is in a hospital room awaiting news that will change his life. We don't know yet in which direction.

Home now, barely inside the door, my dog plops down on the hardwood floor, done for the day, though it is still morning.

My bed beckons me back. I won't resist. I don't have to seize the day, not today, not this day.

I will let it flow over me, a river over a rock. I will see what I can find underwater.

REPAIR

It was distressing to hear
the sound of roofing
until it wasn't—
until the nerve-
shattering ripping of shingles
& hollering &
pounding pounding pounding
of parts into place
became unlikely lullaby
this warm day
me on the couch
listening to it all happen
down the block.

Is this always true
of hard things?

My brother
has promised
when he is well
he will re-
roof the house
Robert & I just bought. He
hasn't laid roof since
that summer a quarter century

ago but he says ours is easy.
A year? he asks. *It'll hold?*
I'm on a ladder
at his house when he asks, righting
vinyl siding disturbed days earlier by
gale-force gusts. He is too
weak & dizzy from chemo
to climb the ladder himself
& I don't tell him
I'm afraid. *It'll hold,* I say, though
I know nothing of structures,
of what crack or fracture
or worn-down middle might
bring bits of sky
or buckets of rain
crashing into my bed.

Half dozing on the couch,
I hear a roofer
singing in a language I don't
know: It'll be alright,
nothing is beyond repair,
& I want to believe him.
I hear now a circular saw,
can almost feel

the rending of what was
to make some-
thing new, can feel
in my self a severance.

MOUNTAIN LION

On the other end of the line, my brother sounds sad, scared, more so than I've heard him sound in decades.

It's in the forties here & gloomy, but where he is it's sunny, seventy, & he's sitting in a rocking chair on his front porch & both of our parents are with him.

He already sounds exhausted though he's only at the beginning of his treatment, not even at the beginning, & there's a long road ahead. I'm exhausted, too, for mostly different reasons, but some of the same. In the past two days I have slept thirty hours.

I hear my brother greet a passing neighbor. I think I hear birds, or maybe I'm imagining the memory of birds. I think I hear my mother eating chevda but that could be a memory, too.

While talking on the phone, I've been staring at a vase on the dresser in my bedroom, white tulips, but I only now see them, see that they are drooping. I'm trying to gear up for a run later, though the moody folk music I've been listening to all morning hasn't done me any favors.

I ask my brother questions, maybe too many questions, maybe all the wrong questions, but I'm concerned. He asks about my toenail. *That was a year ago*, I say, & he says, *I know, I'm just checking*. He is a doctor & my older brother. It's his job to check.

On the other end of the line I hear a neighbor's dog bark, or I think it's a neighbor's dog, the bark is too big to be Brownie's.

Years ago, my brother spotted—one morning, in his meticulously planned housing development with its immaculate lawns, on the crest of a hill—what he claimed was a mountain lion. *Can you imagine?* my mother had asked when she first told me the story.

I thought of the beasts that have shown up at my own door over the years, at all hours, ferocious & starving. But it's just something people say: Can you imagine?

I didn't ask my brother what the lion looked like in the morning light, how it moved across the crest, the sound it made, if it made a sound. I didn't ask what he felt in his chest when he looked in its eyes, when he saw what it was & what it wanted.

THE FIFTH & FINAL HOUSE

At my uncle's funeral, the stories they tell of his life are true, even as other competing stories are also true.

He loved houses, & he & my aunt built all of theirs, four of them, from the ground up, because they wanted (or rather, *he* wanted—he was the picky one) everything to be just so. But the last house, the fifth house, they did not build. They found something he was willing to accept for what it was, kept for twenty-plus years the kitschy Paris-themed window treatments in the kitchen &, in the long hallway, stained glass transoms neither would have selected.

What did it mean to be among the first South Asian immigrants after the Immigration and Nationality Act of 1965 opened things up for non-white settlers? What did it mean for my uncle, my aunt, my own father, my mother, countless relatives & family friends to live at that time in Texas, Kansas, South Carolina, Oklahoma, West Virginia?

I remember the cantaloupe-colored Datsun 240Z my uncle drove from Austin, Texas, to Parkersburg, West Virginia, to meet my aunt for the first time at my parents' brick ranch on Brooklyn Drive with the flowering dogwood out front. I remember a trip to Blackwater Falls, all the ways our brown bodies slick with sweat & mist shone. I remember my aunt's canary yellow crocheted sweater & a gift given to me: a stuffed tiger named Tiger.

At the funeral, hugging my cousin, I keep telling him how very, very proud his father was of him. I whispered the same thing the previous evening, but the way his sobs escalate makes me wonder if I've said the wrong thing. I too know the weight of making immigrant parents proud.

My cousin, a banker, & his wife, a policy analyst, bought their first house a few years ago. Not a house, but a full floor in a converted townhouse on Gramercy Park. For a year, they rented a second apartment while their new place was being renovated. My cousin's wife offered that's why she hadn't read the novel I wrote: it accidentally got packed away in a box that ended up in storage. Sorry.

In Philadelphia, Robert & I are also trying to buy our first house—much more modest than any of my uncle's & aunt's or my cousin's or my parents'—just enough room for us & our badly behaved dog & a guest room for people we love. It's exciting & terrifying & emotional & somehow makes me wonder again & again if I have done in my life things right or wrong & if I have made my parents proud.

In her eulogy, one of my uncle's nieces recalls when she was nineteen, a new immigrant, living for a year with my uncle & aunt (just as my aunt lived with us when she first immigrated) & was struggling to adjust to life in America. She says my uncle gave her advice she never forgot: *When it comes to problems, we are not always meant to find solutions; instead, we are meant to. . .* But I can't catch what comes next because my uncle's niece is crying, the sound system is crackling, the funeral chapel is vast.

I think of that fifth house, the kitschy Paris-themed window treatments my uncle & aunt may have thought they'd remove but never did. My bedroom in my second childhood home, not the one on Brooklyn Drive but the one in North Hills, had—from when we moved in until I left for college & my mother finally replaced them—faux fur curtains the color of Cookie Monster.

In our next house—Robert's & my first house, possibly our last house—what will we change & what will we accept for what it is? What will cover our windows? When will we open the windows & how wide? What shapes will be made by the drapes in the wind & in the middle of the night will we know they are ghosts?

VIII.

ONCE & NEVER

I will never open & sort through
any of those boxes despite
what I may have believed

about myself when I moved
& stored them. The same goes
for the mail in the plastic

basket by the front door
& the bold-faced messages
in my inbox. I will never

wash the reeking dog bed
in the garage, or the stained
dhurrie stuffed in the tattered suitcase,

ancient Samsonite
with tiny wheels decades-dragged
by ancestors back & forth

through Chhatrapati Shivaji Maharaj
International Airport, an electric pink
ribbon affixed to the handle

for ease of identification
so they'd know (as if
they could forget)

which baggage was theirs.
Oh, that they had not claimed it,
allowed it, instead, to sit spinning

on the carousel & had walked, un-
encumbered, out of JFK,
who now would we all be?

When it rains I can
sometimes smell the places
I've never been & glimpse,

through the mist,
the people I once &
never was.

PRAYER

I always forget
the pear tree tucked

behind the hulking mulberry.
And yet each year

it offers me flowers & fruit
as if to forgive,

which is all I've ever wanted.

THE RAIN

For so long I waited
for the rain that when
it came—heavy & unabashed
—I didn't know what

to do, didn't think
to shut the windows,
not even the one
with the borrowed

tomes perched like
exotic birds on the
narrow ledge. I had
gotten so used to

waiting. What now
was I to do? As if
in a Bollywood film,
rush outside wrapped

in a pale sari &, drenched,
dance in a field of flowers?
What would my neighbor
have said had I, in a blur

of blue chiffon, trampled her
exquisite tulips during the down-
pour? Dialed the po-po, or—
is it possible?—raced out

in a summery caftan, this
octogenarian who has seen
over her lifetime God-
knows-what, & joined me?

THE LESS I DO

i spend the day
    dozing, dazed—

rain on the skylight,
    the march sky

a film screen before
    the opening credits,

a thick novel splayed open
    beside me

on the block print bedspread
    —spine up, pages down—

its secrets
    for another day.

i know creekside
    among the brown leaves

the snowdrops' heads are bowed
    in prayer. and beneath the

tulip poplar the crocuses
    are clearing their throats

to sing their hymn
 of coming spring.

i don't have to do a thing
 to make this happen.

rain will fall, wild-
 flowers will bloom.

i don't have to do a thing
 to make this happen.

the less i do
 the louder the birds

in the hedgerow sing.

SMALL BOAT

Two mandarins
in a deep blue bowl—
sunrise, sunset.

On the windowsill
against the gray winter day,
the red amaryllis.

Two mandarins
in a deep blue bowl—
laughter & joy.

In a red silk shawl,
the amaryllis sings
"Lutf Woh Ishq Mein."

Two mandarins
in a deep blue bowl—
ritual & breath.

In day's last light
the amaryllis glows—a winged
creature, a whispered prayer.

The deep blue bowl:
a small boat.
No one is alone.

MORNING PRAYER

What does it feel like
this autumn morning
pen on paper
a pale pear on the butcher block
& all the while the dance of
shadows & light on the cream-
colored wall?
I often ask but rarely answer.
What does it feel like
to be alive?
Don't make yet another list.
Say & let settle
one thing true:
  Wind-loosened,
the maple leaf—
bright as a flame,
red as a heart—
savors the fall.

I DON'T REMEMBER THE RAIN

I don't remember the rain
but the woods are soaked
as if it's poured for days.
It's been like this for me

lately: weeks, months, even
years an inky blur.
Have I not been present
to the world around me?

Then how to explain
the red berries exploding
in the morning light that stopped
me & made me sigh

or the cardinal in the yard
or the winged seed glittering?
Was that last week
or last year?

The path is muddy
but it feels good
to sink a little.

Through the winter trees
I can see the quiet road in
the distance & for a moment
I think it's a river—

& maybe it once was
or will be.

I've made more mistakes
than I'm willing to admit.

Tomorrow or in years
I will look at the dried mud
caked thick on my blue sneakers
& wonder how I made it through.

IX.

REJOICE

The stranger on the sidewalk says to his dog, who has paused to sniff me, *Come along, Bud; that's not a deer.* But I hear "dear" and want to say, *Oh, but I am,* and in fact had written that very morning in my notebook a letter to myself that began, *Dear One, I'm sorry today is difficult for you. I know that you are suffering.*

December, and the trees in the woods and the dark still stream are whispering, *Shh,* are whispering, *Honor the season, honor death,* but the bright lights on the green trees in the tall windows of neighbors' houses are blinking, *Celebrate,* are blinking, *Rejoice.* And perhaps it is this dissonance that has rubbed me raw.

Dear One, it is okay to celebrate solitude. Celebrate, Darling, the rest you'll find, these long dark days, in this safe cave—that is, the fourth-floor flat you've done your best to make a nest, never mind the mice and pile of perpetually dirty laundry on the bedroom floor. Rejoice, Jaanam, in the cold, hard earth inside of which something is unbecoming and quietly making itself—(a miracle!)—anew.

THE SONG

When danger approaches, sing to it.
ARABIAN PROVERB, QUOTED IN AMY HEMPEL'S *SING TO IT*

My mother has a terrible voice, but she was the only one who knew all the words so she sang the loudest.

By terrible I mean the sound of uncooked rice being poured into a stainless steel dabba.

By terrible I mean the color of dry leaves on the forest floor in winter at dusk.

Thursdays we'd gather in front of the small altar on the low table in my parents' bedroom in West Virginia, ring a bell—a replica of the Liberty Bell, though none of us had been to Philadelphia—and sing songs of devotion.

Twameva mata.

Om jai jagdish sharaya.

Shree rama rama rameth.

My brother and I mumbled. My father whispered. My mother, though not particularly religious, roared.

Then there was the Lowrey electric organ bought from the mall with preset rhythms for samba and rhumba and waltz and sound effects for flute, strings, horn, and a button for vibrato. Money was so tight back then, I don't know that my father would have agreed to the purchase had my mother not said the organ was for my brother and me so we could Learn Music, so we could be Well-Rounded Candidates when it was time to apply for College. We barely touched it.

Evenings, after long, difficult days, my mother would go into the organ room, a bird on her shoulder, and play.

And squawk.

Seventy-six trombones led the big parade.

I could have danced all night.

It's cherry pink and apple blossom white.

Now it is more than thirty years later. I have had a long, difficult day of my own. The world has. It is April and I am walking my dog in my neighborhood—Philadelphia; I finally made it here!—and down the street the sakuras are pink puffs of cotton candy and in our yard the apple tree is erupting. I hear my mother's voice singing to me. It is the smell of blossoms on the breeze.

WE WILL SING

We wanted to
bring home
all that
followed us:
the dog that followed us
the child that followed us
the cat that followed us
the snake that followed us
the river that followed us
the rock that followed us
the cloud that followed us
the song that followed us
the air of loss and of possibility that followed us.
We wanted to gather them all
at the american consulate,
get them all visas
and international flights,
to be able to have
our magnetic
charm and desirability
affirmed at will
and endlessly
in our small apartment
stateside.
The dog would have worms
we knew,
the child would require

shots and a nanny
and shelves of tissues
to wipe its nose,
the river would demand
a bigger backyard,
and the cloud would
bring monsoons that
would drown the
summer sun. But the
song. The song
we will sing
in every room,
out every window,
in every shower,
we will make
up words,
write new
lyrics, a new bridge,
the neighbors will hear the song
our coworkers will hear the song
our friends will hear the song
our family will hear the song
our bigoted aunt who we have to endure
every New Year's Eve will hear the song
and when the
snake strikes
or the cat scratches
or the rock falls
or the air presses down
like hot daggers,
we will sing
we will sing
we will sing.

THE POEMS I NEVER WROTE

live in a small house
they built at the edge
of the woods
I run through
regularly.
The site,
mossy and
green and serenaded
by a creek that knows
the chords and lyrics
to every Kishore Kumar
song, was chosen by the
poem about my
father's uncanny ability
to purchase a case
of perfect mangoes
every summer
in West Virginia,
and the structure
was designed by the poem
about the first boy
I kissed, though
the task of overseeing
construction fell
mostly to the poem
about the woman in my office
who went out for coffee

and never came back,
my shame in not
naming the bruises I'd
noticed on her neck
and arms, the
pair of heels and
salami sandwich she
left in her desk drawer.
(I should note,
the poem
about the darkness
that night
my freshman year
in college did help
decorate and
hang artwork,
as did the poem
about the police officer
in 2002 who
told me he could make me
disappear.)
I've never been
inside the house,
yet I know, though
the house looks small,
the rooms
are vast and
innumerable.
Sometimes,
when I run by, I tip
my head or wave,
especially if I notice
one of the poems, say,

the one about the neighborhood
cats my mother feeds,
peeking out of a window,
or if I glimpse some of the poems
hanging laundry
as the many poems
titled "Morning Prayer"
are wont to do, often
together, often
joined by the poem
that can never be
seen except in
shadows.
The laundry, after all, is washed
in their tears
and they
like to watch the water
evaporate, to study
the patterns of salt
left behind.
But mostly, I
try my best to
respect their
privacy, to run on
by, to avert my
eyes, to forget about
the house entirely.
The poems who live there
have made it clear
they are none of my
business, at least
for now, and they
have work to do.

LAYING IT DOWN (REPRISE)

The spring leaves.
   The rain.
  The branches swaying.
        A solo cello, plaintive
& unsentimental, on the
classical station: the sound
   of blood and breath.
  Did I say rain?
  Did I say orange parrot
       tulips, extravagant
      & without shame?
  Surely I described
its wet petals, &, above,
     the spring leaves,
the swaying branches?
  Did I impart the drum
     & thrum of rain
       on the roof
all through the night
  & into the day?
The ducks are dancing.
  The slug is dancing.
   The frog is dancing.
Ganesh is dancing.
  The branches are dancing.
  I am swaying.

I am praying.
  Surely I described
 my wet cheeks.
Did I say:
  The radiator hisses?
the wind moans?
  the neighbors' husky
 whimpers & whines?
  Did I describe
 —adequately
& with all the right words
  so you could hear,
really hear, in your own
  body—the sound of
  my heart howl?

MORNING PRAYER

Pull back the curtain.
Let the sun slap
    the kitchen counter-cum-altar-cum-
        craft center-cum-escritoire-cum-confessional.
    Let the smell of ripening
        quince orphaned from
    the fruit bowl & arranged among
            other sacred things—
                a feather, a river stone,
                    a marble the gold of dandelion
                    after an April downpour—
    rise & wrap around you.
        The rocks
            you brought this morning
                from the frost-pocked yard
            carry within them
                    the moon,
                    the vast dark night,
                        &
                        stars.
            Know that everything is
                before you.

MY NEXT BOOK

My mother
saw my next
book in a dream,
she tells me,
but when I press
her for details
she has none.
Title? Genre?
Color of cover?
She doesn't remember,
or so she claims.
Well, I sigh, *in your
next dream please
take notes.*
No can do,
she says.
*But know:
it's all there;
it is already written.*

ACKNOWLEDGMENTS

Sincere gratitude to the editors of the following publications, in which these pieces first appeared.

> *Cherry Tree*: "race point," "We Will Sing"
> *The Georgia Review*: "Seeds," "My Birthright"
> *Kenyon Review Online*: "Tunnels"
> *The Margins*: "Ghazal"
> *The Massachusetts Review*: "Copper Beech"
> *swamp pink* (formerly *Crazyhorse*): "Rejoice"

"Morning Prayer" ("Pull back the curtain. . .") was included in a chapbook curated by visual artist Clarity Haynes and published in conjunction with her *Altar-ed Bodies* show at Denny Dimin Gallery in New York City in early 2020.

"Tunnels" was reprinted in the anthology *Ways of Walking* (New Door Books, 2022), edited by Ann de Forest.

The poem "Ghazal" will be printed in a future issue of *The Margins*, the digital magazine of the Asian American Writers' Workshop.

Thank you to all the wonderful folks at UPK and especially to my editor, Abby Freeland, for steadfastly believing in this book; to Kasey Jueds and Joshua Jennifer Espinoza, for their generous and enormously helpful feedback; and to Dilruba Ahmed, Purvi Shah, and Kazim Ali, for taking time to read the finished manuscript and to offer such kind words of support.

NOTES ON THE TEXT

"My Birthright": I believe that what I write about my father and fear is true, even as the exact opposite is also true. My father is one of the bravest, most fearless people I have ever known. The phrase "I want to tell about fire" comes from artwork by Eve Fowler.

"longboat key": The dancer mentioned is Marion Ramírez.

"after a poem by james wright": The Wright poem referenced is "Lying in a Hammock at William Duffy's Farm in Pine Island, Minnesota."

"Why We Woke Too Early": The title is a reference to Mary Oliver's "Why I Wake Early." Oliver is one of my favorite poets and her influence is woven throughout this collection. The structure of this poem is influenced by Richard Siken's "Why."

"three of cups": The dancer mentioned is Blakeney Bullock.

"race point": The poet mentioned is Eileen Myles.

"The Birds": The turn at the end of the second section probably owes something to Mary Oliver, as does much in this collection.

"Before & After": The Jean Valentine poem quoted is "From the Questions of Bhanu Kapil," which is built on questions from Kapil's *The Vertical Interrogation of Strangers.*

"The Fifth & Final House": The title is a play on Jhumpa Lahiri's short story "The Third and Final Continent." This poem is written in loving memory of Dinesh Chandra Mehta.

"The Song": I have taken poetic license. My mother sings like an angel.

ABOUT THE AUTHOR

Rahul Mehta is the author of the novel *No Other World* and the short story collection *Quarantine*. Their work has received a Lambda Literary Award and an Asian American Literary Award and has appeared in numerous publications, including the *Kenyon Review*, the *Massachusetts Review*, the *Georgia Review*, *The Sun*, and the *New York Times Magazine*. Born and raised in West Virginia in a Gujarati-American household, they currently live in Philadelphia with their partner and their dog.